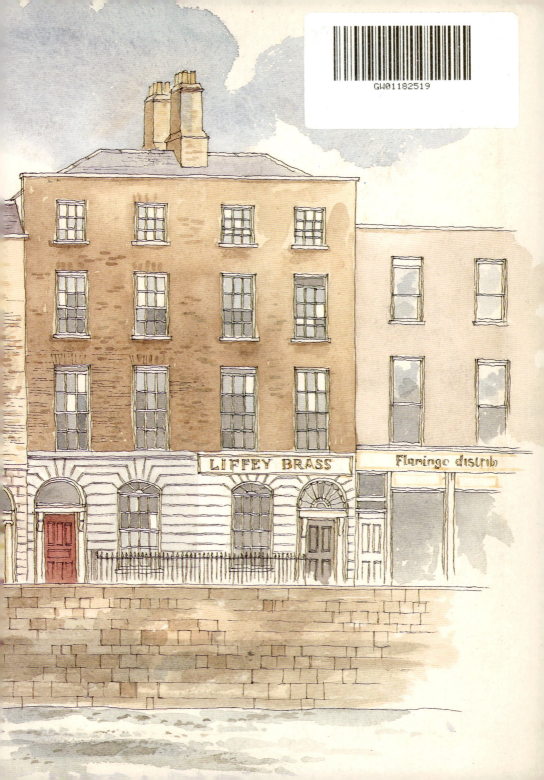

IRELAND

An Illustrated Address Book

Appletree Press

First published and printed by The Appletree Press Ltd,
7 James Street South, Belfast BT2 8DL.
All rights reserved. No part of this publication may be
reproduced or transmitted in any form or by any
means, electronic or mechanical, photocopying,
recording or any information and retrieval system,
without prior permission in writing from
The Appletree Press Ltd.

ISBN 0 86281 294 1

Front cover: Royal Hospital, Kilmainham, Dublin

Back cover: Seezer's Butcher Shop,
Thomas Street, Dublin

Illustrations: Kieran Doyle O'Brien
Captions: Vincent Caprani, Renagh Holohan,
Marcus Patton

A
B

Round House
Cobh, Co. Cork

Probably no town in Ireland has been the scene of such sorrow as has Cobh. It was here that thousands of Irish men and women said goodbye to their families and sailed for the New World. Most never returned. The charming town, formerly Queenstown and noted for its large cathedral, steep hills and beautiful location, has for several centuries been a centre for Atlantic sea travel. Since famine days and during the heyday of luxury crossings earlier this century, transatlantic liners called regularly at Cobh; now the QE II picks up passengers for the leisure cruise to New York only a few times a year. The Royal Cork Yacht Club, founded in 1720 and the oldest in the world, was located here until recently.

Kenny's Bookshop
High Street/Middle Street, Galway

One of the best-known landmarks in Galway, Kenny's, which has been in one family for more than 50 years, is located in greatly expanded and rambling premises that run back to back between High Street and Middle Street. The bookshop is a popular browsing place for those seeking antiquarian books, maps and prints, as well as works by contemporary Irish authors. The bookshop building dates from the sixteenth century and was a pub earlier this century. The art gallery, as illustrated, specialises in Irish artists and sculptors. The four circular objects between the windows are shallow wicker baskets.

City Hall
Donegall Square, Belfast

The elaborate Edwardian seat of Belfast Council and its offices dominates the city from its island site at the top of Royal Avenue. Built by Sir Brumwell Thomas between 1902 and 1906, when the city was a thriving industrial port, it replaced the eighteenth-century White Linen Hall. Statues of Queen Victoria and of a former Mayor, Sir Edward Harland MP (co-founder of what at one time was the biggest ship building firm in the world and the employer of 12,000 people in Belfast by 1914), stand on the surrounding lawn. This is the east porch and it was modelled on the porch of Gibbs' Street, Mary le Strand, in London.

Farmhouse near Anascaul, Co. Kerry

There are farmhouses like this all over the country: two-storey, plain, frugal and slated. Most have never been modernised but were considered quite advanced when compared to the poorer thatched cottages of their day. Anascaul, on the Dingle Peninsula (where this cottage stands in its own neat garden), is a tiny village noted for its striking views. There are a number of ancient monuments in the vicinity.

JKL

The Stag's Head
Dame Court, Dublin

The following report appeared in a Dublin newspaper on 3 October 1895: 'On the site of an old Dublin hostelry in Dame Lane, a palatial bar has just been completed for Mr G W Tyson... entirely rebuilt and fitted in the most modern and complete manner as to style, finish and equipment, it will bear comparison with the best establishments of its kind either in London or in any other part of England. The "Stag's Head", as the building is called, is chiefly of County Dublin red brick, with a front of chiselled limestone richly moulded and carved.'

George's Quay
Cork

Cork is full of quays as the city encompasses an island in the River Lee, where early tenth-century Norsemen first settled. The houses here at George's Quay are early eighteenth century and typical of many of the city's riverside buildings. They are of several different styles and their ground floors are used for a myriad of purposes. Many similar buildings, with interesting and unique features, have been demolished in recent years and others have suffered from unsympathetic improvements.

Carlow Railway Station
Carlow

Irish railway stations tend to be in three main styles: Italianate, such as Heuston (formerly Kingsbridge) in Dublin; Gothic, such as in Portlaoise; or Jacobean, as with this one in Carlow. The line from Dublin was opened in 1846 and the station itself was designed in brown brick with granite dressings by Sir John MacNeill, who was also responsible for the other stations on the route. Carlow was originally a terminus and coaches ran from here to Kilkenny, Clonmel and Waterford during the nineteenth century. The evening train from Dublin, which took two-and-a-half hours to reach Carlow, connected with the mail coach for Cork and arrived there at 5 a.m. the next morning.

House Front
Shipquay Street, Derry

Granted to the citizens of London by James I in 1613, Derry was planted with Protestant settlers and surrounded by a thick wall, much of which still stands. This house dates from after the great siege of 1689 when a superior Jacobite force failed to take the city, an event which is commemorated by loyalists in Northern Ireland to this day. Shipquay is one of the four principal streets leading from each of the gates, and as can be seen from the picture of this house with an antique shop in the basement, it is exceptionally steep. George Farquhar, the playwright, whose works include *The Beaux Stratagem* and *The Recruiting Officer*, was born on Shipquay Street.

Clockmaker's Shop
Fownes Street, Dublin

Fownes Street is part of the Temple Bar area, Dublin's self-proclaimed Left Bank. The street preserves little more than the name of Alderman Fownes, who leased land for development purposes back in the 1650s from the Dublin Corporation. Nevertheless, it still retains the charm of the many little streets which were laid out about that time, between Dame Street and the river, and which survive, although largely rebuilt in the eighteenth century. The old clockmaker's shop, with its display of fine timepieces, alas, has not withstood modernisation — '...for Time is no Time when Time is past'.

The Kitchen Bar
Victoria Square, Belfast

For many years this pub stood alongside the Imperial Colosseum Music Hall, which became the Buffalo Hotel and Music Hall, and finally the Empire Theatre before it was demolished. At this prime location for night life, one William Cowan established 'bonded stores' when the building was put up in 1879. Thomas Conlon was running his Kitchen Bar a few doors away in Victoria Square and moved here in 1892. By Victorian standards this was quite a restrained pub, but its ornamental lettering, the chamfered edges to the windows, and the cut-away corner, all promise comfortable drinking inside.

X Y Z

Cottages
Ramelton, Co. Donegal

This 'planter' town was settled by Scotch Presbyterians early in the seventeenth century when the land was granted to the first Baron Stewart. His descendant still lives in the village, where he builds boats, but Fort Stewart, the plantation castle three miles to the east, is no longer in family hands. Today a quiet fishing port on Lough Swilly and dormitory town for Letterkenny, Ramelton was the birthplace of the Reverend Francis Makemie, founder of the Presbyterian church in the United States. The Old Meeting House, where he no doubt worshipped before leaving for America in 1682, is being restored by a local ecumenical committee. There are some fine, small Georgian buildings here.